Getting Around

By Bicycle

Cassie Mayer

www.heinemann.co.uk/library
Visit our website to find out more information about **Heinemann Library** books.

To order:
☎ Phone 44 (0) 1865 888066
▤ Send a fax to 44 (0) 1865 314091
▭ Visit the Heinemann Bookshop at www.heinemann.co.uk/library to browse our
catalogue and order online.

First published in Great Britain by Heinemann Library,
Halley Court, Jordan Hill, Oxford OX2 8EJ, part of
Harcourt Education. Heinemann is a registered trademark
of Harcourt Education Ltd.

Editorial: Tracey Crawford, Cassie Mayer, Dan Nunn, and
Sarah Chappelow
Design: Jo Hinton-Malivoire
Picture Research: Tracy Cummins
Production: Duncan Gilbert

Originated by Chroma Graphics (Overseas) Pte. Ltd
Printed and bound in China by South China
Printing Company

10 digit ISBN 0 431 18216 7
13 digit ISBN 978 0 431 18216 2

10 09 08 07 06
10 9 8 7 6 5 4 3 2 1

British Library Cataloguing in Publication Data
Mayer, Cassie
Getting around by bicycle
1.Cycling - Juvenile literature
I.Title
388.3'472

Acknowledgements
The publishers would like to thank the following for
permission to reproduce photographs:
Corbis pp. **4** (Macduff Everton), **5** (Michel
Philippot/Sygma), **8** (Tom & Dee Ann McCarthy), **10**
(Strauss/Curtis), **12** (Peter Turnley), **13** (Tibor Bognar), **15**
(Duomo), **16** (Peter Turnley), **17** (Paul W. Liebhardt), **18**
(S. Andreas/Zefa), **20** (Herve Claude/ Sygma), **22** (Royalty
Free), **23** (unicyclist, Strauss/Curtis); Getty Images pp. **6**
(Chesley), **7** (Morris), **9** (Bilow), **11** (Neleman), **14** (photo
& co), **19** (Lemmens), **21** (Francis), **23** (family cycling,
photo & co), **23** (rickshaw, Neleman).

Cover image of cyclists on the beach in Zanzibar
reproduced with permission of Gideon Mendel. Back
cover image of children reproduced with permission of
Tibor Bognar/Corbis.

Every effort has been made to contact copyright holders
of any material reproduced in this book. Any omissions
will be rectified in subsequent printings if notice is given
to the publishers.

The paper used to print this book comes from sustainable
resources.

Contents

Getting around by bicycle

Every day people move from place to place.

Some people move by bike.

What bikes carry

Some bikes carry passengers.

Some bikes carry things.

How bikes move

wheel

Bikes have two wheels.

pedal

You push the pedals to move the wheels.

unicycle

This is a unicycle.
It has only one wheel.

rickshaw

This is a rickshaw.
It has three wheels.

How people use bikes

People ride bikes to work.

Children ride bikes to school.

Some people ride bikes for exercise.

Some people ride bikes to race.

People ride bikes in cities.

People ride bikes in the country.

Some people ride bikes for fun.

Some people ride bikes for work.

A bike can take you to many places.

And a bike can take you home.

Bike vocabulary

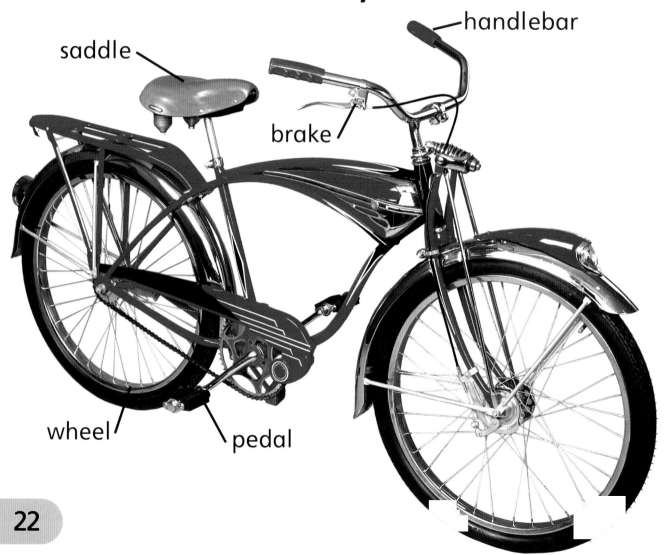

saddle

handlebar

brake

wheel

pedal

22

Picture glossary

 **exercise** keeping your body fit to stay healthy

 **rickshaw** a bike with three wheels that is used to carry people

 **unicycle** a bike with one wheel

Index

Notes to Parents and Teachers
Before reading
Talk about riding a bike. Can they ride a two-wheeled bike? Where do they like to go on their bike?
Talk about the wheels, the pedals, the handlebars, the brakes, and the saddle.
Talk about different sorts of bikes e.g. tricycle, unicycle, tandem.

After reading
Make a simple book. Ask children to draw a picture of a unicycle, a bicycle, and a tricycle. They should draw around a disc for the wheels. Discuss with them how to write: This has one wheel. This has two wheels. This has three wheels.

Counting in twos: Give children a pile of model wheels. How many bicycles could they make?

Sing a song (to the tune "John Brown's Body"):
"I rode into town on my old bicycle." (3 times)
"But a wheel fell off and I fell down and landed on the ground." (Children act out wobbling, falling off, and lying on the floor.)
Chorus: "Who will help me mend my old bicycle?" (3 times)
"Put the wheel on, pump it up, and then I can ride again." (Children join in actions.)

Titles in the *Getting Around* series include:

Hardback 0-431-18222-1

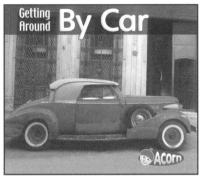

Hardback 0-431-18218-3

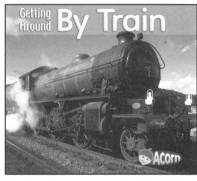

Hardback 0-431-18221-3

Hardback 0-431-18216-7

Hardback 0-431-18217-5

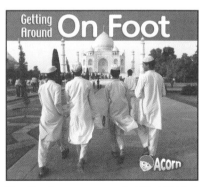

Hardback 0-431-18219-1

Find out about other titles from Heinemann Library on our website www.heinemann.co.uk/library